SALTY
Poems from the Sea

Inspiration on the fly
Published by PoemCatcher Creations
Salisbury Centre
2 Salisbury Road
Edinburgh, EH16 5AB

www.poemcatcher.com

Copyright
All the poems in this book were donated with love and permission to be published. It would be thievery to steal the copyright from the authors themselves. It remains their own.
This is their beautiful creativity and I am just a creative collator.

Sincere thanks to all who made me feel so welcome.

Cover design by Trevor at Fresh Digital

Use of this material is welcomed – providing it inspires, engages and enthrals audiences.
Each and every poem in this book is brilliant. If you disagree, send £10 with your complaint to a child in Haiti.

"SALTY"
ISBN 978-0-9566018-9-6

Be proud to own it!
Excellent beach reading

Hidden Treasures

Treasures lurk here
Beneath the ink
Of young and old
Between the pages
of creation
timelessly waiting
your exploration.

Turn another page
Or dwell

About the Mess

Think, feel, doodle, make a list, ~~scratch some lines out~~, start again, find more paper, talk to your friends, gather ideas, just look around. They are here to be found.

Many of you did,
believed that you could
You did brilliant
I knew that you would
I love your first efforts
With edits and all
The edge of creation
A little bit raw.

P.S. this book is full of mistakes. Such is life.
Some are mine, some are yours.
I don't mind.
The struggle for perfectionism ain't worth the stress.
I far prefer a creative mess.

£2 per book goes to charity

SOS Children's Villages provides a family for life for children who have lost their parents through war, famine, disease, natural disaster and poverty. Over 78,000 orphaned and abandoned children are cared for by SOS mothers in clusters of family homes in more than 500 of our unique Children's Villages in 124 countries worldwide. Thousands more children benefit from SOS Children's outreach support which includes education, vocational training, medical care and community development programmes. SOS Children also provides emergency relief in situations of crisis and disaster, and continues to support families in earthquake and tsunami-affected countries.

Registered Charity Number 1069204
www.soschildrensvillages.org.uk

Contents

- RISING TIDE 11
  - A Nameless Villanelle 12
  - Sunday School trip in the 50's 14
  - Fringe by the Sea 15
  - Indispensable Man 16
  - Alastair's poem (age 8) 18
  - Andrew's Circular Poem 19
  - Eyes in the sky 20
  - North Berwick is a great place 21
  - Salty NB 22
  - A view from the Lower Quay 23
  - Tent 24
  - Hugh's Ditty 25
  - My Sea 25
  - Beeches above the Law 27
  - BALISEUR 29
  - North Berwick in August 31
- HISTORIC WALK 33
  - Family Day out 40
  - Rugged Ralph 41
  - Wonderful William 41
  - ESP 42
  - 3 Legged Dog 42

The Spiegeltent 43

Waves 43

Oh, North Berwick 44

Untitled 44

The Big Yella Thing 45

In My Caravan 45

Sea Shore 46

Our house in the middle of the street 47

Rain 48

N.O.R.T.H. B.E.R.W.I.C.K. 49

The annoying boy 50

Berwick's Law 51

Sunstroke 52

Red Kite 53

Pride and Joy 54

Fred McCauley 55

The Quintessential North Berwick Limerick 56

Visiting 56

The Sun in North Berwick 57

My Favoraite Place 58

AHOY! – North Berwick 59

Fringe by the Sea 60

Maisie's Boat 61

Simply the Best 62

Off key 63
From Submarine to the Moon 64
The Big Tent " North Berwick Harbour 64
Hugh's 2nd Ditty 65
NB Shore 66
Bunfight 67
North Berwick 68
Raj 69
See 69
North Berwick Highland Games 70
Jelly Belly 72
The Place to be 73
Fishy Face Rap 74
Morning World 75
The Sea by Camper 76
"Fringe Fun" 77
Getting the Fringe benefits 78
The reluctant performer 79
S.A.L.T.Y. 80
Sitting by the Sea 81
Rant 82
Get Up 83
Love & Money 84
Life in Marly Green 85

The Spiegel Prayer 86

By The Sea 86

Saturdays 87

North Berwick 88

Del Sol 89

Harr 89

Alan's Poem 90

Local Input 90

Bass Rock Birds 91

High Times 91

Seashell 92

We stayed in a flat… 93

Tippecanoe 94

Another poem found 95

Keep Smiling Through 96

Jean Florette 96

Raise your hem FC Ukelele 97

CATCH OF THE DAY 98

Mushrooms 99

My Honey 100

First Hotdog in Space 101

Toast to a "Steak Bake" 102

Meat 103

BEE & FAMILY 105

Untitled 107
"Summer!" 108
Moving 109
Glitter 110
The Day Centre, North Berwick 111
Far out to Sea 112
Nibble 113
GOLF 114
The Great Game of Golf 115
Golf in the Sun 116
Golf 118
ROMANCE 119
David and Amy's Page 120
Charlie 121
Tulips 122
A poem to writing 123
This place 124
OUTGOING TIDE 125
Nap time 126
Write another poem here… 127
List of Poets 128
OTHER POEMCATCHER BOOKS 129

RISING TIDE

A Nameless Villanelle

Do not go gentle into city bright
Like moths attracted to unfettered flame
When summer days give way to autumn night.

Turn not your back on Law's unchallenged height
Or Bass Rock's craggy home to *Sula* fame
Do not go gentle into city bright.

Fair Scottish divas sang to gentle light
Till sleep and purest pleasure overcame
When summer days give way to autumn night.

Where waves lap languid on the shingle white
Where culture, coastal fringe to North Sea came
Do not go gentle into city bright.

Pause only, challenged soul, some verse to write
Let not the poem catcher miss his aim
When summer days give way to autumn night.

Do not in urban edifice excite
Nor bury self in fickle fancy's game
Do not go gentle into city bright
When summer days give way to autumn night.

By Lyle Crawford

From Lyle Crawford
To a PoemCatcher

Coming out of Barbara Dickson Concert on Friday night, you challenged me for a villanelle. The attached, with apologies, is my best effort in 3 hours! (obviously based on the villanelle "Do not go gentle into that good night" which is also nameless)

It is intended as appreciation of "Fringe by the Sea", and also of the song "The gentle light that wakes me" first recorded by Phil Cunningham (the composer) and Duncan Chisholm, who both appeared at FBTS

Lyle Crawford

Sunday School trip in the 50's

Have you ever tasted "cod and chips"
At the end of those sea-side trips
Remember salt and vinegar an' the newspaper bag
And to wipe your lips before your fag.

Two an six bought a "kiss me quick"
You ate candyfloss til you were sick
Pennies in the slot machines to win a Woodbine
A paddle in the sea , and then you were fine.

Sand in your shoes and some in your toes
The smells of the seaside attacking your nose
The last minute shop, something for Mum
Late for the train, I'll now have to run

By David Farmery. Chirnside, Berwickshire.

Fringe By The Sea

Nothing quite like it!
Offering
Rest and excitement
There in the town and down by the shore;
Harbour setting for music and art, plus

Bookwriter's tales.
Everyone's tastes in a
Rich cornucopia of
Wonderful ways to fill in your days.
Ice cream, fish suppers, all
Come together in a colourful festival
Known as *"**Fringe By The Sea**"*

Ronald Peebles

Indispensable Man

My wife and I have recently moved back to North Berwick after some forty years , work having taken us over that period the length and breadth of the country. At about the age of seventeen a local man namely Norrie Wayne, a drummer with the North Berwick pipe band recited a poem to me that I have never forgot and I have taken it with me through life , by an unknown poet it has a fantastic and very meaningful message one that I believe many people could learn from.

Alex Ralston

THE INDISPENSIBLE MAN.

SOME TIME WHEN YOUR FEELING IMPORTANT.
SOME TIME WHEN YOUR EGOS IN BLOOM.
SOME TIME WHEN YOU TAKE IT FOR GRANTED YOUR THE
BEST EDUCATD MAN IN THE ROOM.
SOME TIME WHEN YOU FEEL THAT YOUR GOING WOULD
LEAVE AN UNFITABLE HOLE.
JUST FOLLOW THIS SIMPLE INSTRUCTION AND SEE HOW IT
HUMBLES YOUR SOLE

TAKE A BUCKET AND FILL IT WITH WATER .
PUT YOUR HANDS IN IT UP TO THEIR WRISTS.
PULL THEM OUT AND THE HOLE THAT REMAINS THERE IS A
MEASURE OF HOW YOU'LL BE MISSED.

YOU MAY SPLASH ALL YOU LIKE WHEN YOU ENTER.
YOU MAY STIR UP THE WATER GALORE.
BUT STOP AND YOU'LL FIND IN A MOMENT THAT
THE WATERS THE SAME AS BEFORE.

NOW THE MORAL TO THIS IS QUITE SIMPLE.
DO YOUR BEST MY GOOD FRIEND WHILE YOU CAN.
WITH A SMILE AND A JOKE AND BE GENTLE.
FOR THERES NO INDISPENSIBLE MAN

Alastair's poem (age 8)

North Berwick is sunny when,
Fringe by the sea comes to town,
I can see Bass Rock and just a
bit too much sea!

By Alastair – Age 8

By Alastair (age 8)

Andrew's Circular Poem

By Andrew Newman

Eyes in the sky

Eyes in the sky

Gliders in the sky
Mesmorised as they fly so high
Near and far
like Eyes in the sky
They watch as the sun slowly sets

By Miss Blossom

North Berwick is a great place

Nb is a great place to be it may not have Jb or even Jay-Z but it has friendly people and parks so come to Nb got the beach and the sea

By Lauren Watt

Salty NB

Will that be salt or sauce?
We pondered for a moment
Were we in the East?
Or in the West?
Perhaps some vinegar and a pickle
Oh what a dilemma

Eeh just salt please
What fun in North Berwick
Down by the Sea
Where the seagulls fly West
To keep the sand from their eyes.

What a magical place
This jewel of the East

By M.C.

A view from the Lower Quay

Its lots of fun when you're young
    By the sea

It's a diddle in the middle
    When you piddle in the sea

It's bloody cold when you're old
    By the sea

The birds and the fish make a really nice dish
    When you're cooking by the sea

By John Dory

Tent

```
      T
     HE
    SPEE
    E EEE
   GLETEM
  T HOW THAT
  SWHAT ICALL
  AM ERECTION
       ||
```

MARLENE EDINBURGH
NOT SO MUCH OLD PULTENEY
NEXT TIME.

By David Murdoch

Hugh's Ditty

Fringe by the Sea
Is where you should be
Wonderful shows from morning to night
Adults and children all thrilled with delight

By Hugh Trevor

My Sea

Sea, Sea
Come wash over me
Wash my mind clear of the day,
Wash it away.

Sun, Sun
Shine on me
Shine on me by the Sea

By Ally Scott

BEECHES ABOVE THE LAW

From tough Scots sod,
sheltered on the Law's long crag
from Lowland wind's eternal
impatience, they dug out room
for sixteen beeches.

With the hopeful coming
of that spring, following long
Stuart winter, they unsaddled
rieving stirrups and planted
peace.

The Union was
fact. These trees grew
to represent it, beeches
lofting foreign above
clumped Scots whin.

They shadowed bondagers
straining through schaws, carrying
their hope in small bundles
off to waiting ships, further
than any local horizon.

Their leaves grew golden
with autumn, a newly tourist town
lazily stretching out below
to swallow up
empty fields.

New wind tugs at them,
restless as ever. Thin ground
is still not home to elegant
roots, grown gnarled
from holding rock.

Now six are down, rotting
beneath the bursting yellow
whin in bloom. Ten silver skeletons
guard their last view over
a wind-whipped Forth.

December 1993

Beeches above the Law

By David Berry

*I don't usually include 'old' poems in my collection,
But it seems apt to allow a local historian to submit
One of his dusty treasures.*

BALISEUR

Je suis la lampe qui me guide
　　　　—Pierre Réverdy

The night slips
from the finger. I ascend
the careful stair, as in a ritual
to confront the day.
The sky takes shape around the platform
in that breathless moment when the light
has swept up the last star
and the real world stops
turning. The day and I
regard each other
like uncertain enemies.

When the sky speaks
blue to the water, its tongue
rolls around the fisted rock,
the gashed knuckles of its lone finger.
The spoken blue has no word
for this, only hints
at the thin coast of Brittany
that will sometimes surface
as if looking for us.

Other days, the sea and the sky
clamp their jaws together
steamily intimate
with the lantern glass. The silence
weighs cathedral-quiet, as if
measuring the sins of night.

Only at night do the waves become
the sleek and bottomless
floor of the world. The ceilingless
temple of sky is black with banners
and a snow of stars. The blade of lantern
sweeps colour through the thickest wind.
Fist and finger poke defiance at the night.
The light booms a silent answer,
defining where we shall look—
what we shall see,
or not see.

By Dave Berry
October 1980

North Berwick in August

Sitting listening to some summer tunes
The gentle breeze welcome
Surrounded by sand and sea
I'm as happy as can be

Fishing nets, buckets and spades
Flags fluttering in the wind
Ice cream at the seaside
We're so lucky to be able to enjoy this.

By Ali Buchanan

HISTORIC WALK

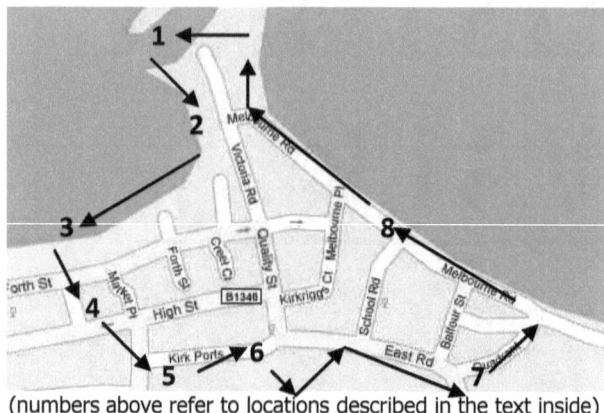

(numbers above refer to locations described in the text inside)

Welcome to a walk of less than an hour around a picturesque seaside town that has re-invented itself more times than have most cities.

By Dave Berry

Part of Fringe by the Sea 2010

Images taken from Bruce Jamieson's *North Berwick in Old Picture Postcards*, published by Zaltbommel/Netherlands, 1985
© David S. Berry   Revision C — August 11th 2010

Harbour (1) *(re-cross green, down broad steps)* Originally a natural haven created by pophyrite lava flows of Platcock Rocks, the earliest constructed part of the harbour is the uncemented stone of the North Pier, held in place by wooden chocks. These need to be replaced every decade. Nothing remains of the original quays and buildings, also of wood. As well as pilgrims, trade was carried on with the Baltic and Low Countries. Many pantiles found across East Lothian arrived as ballast. With the agricultural revolution, new granaries were built to store potatoes, oats, etc for export. In 1812, a major rebuilding of the harbour was undertaken by the Stevenson family. Note the intricate masonry whose precision came from workmen's skills in lighthouses. The railway created a boom in fishing until the herring fished out post-WWI. Galloway's Pier was built for paddle steamers to serve a late Victorian boom in seaside holidays— the East Coast equivalent of *"doon the watter".*

Redguantlet calls at Galloway's Pier, 1912

Old Kirk (2) *(across green from SSC Entrance)* During the 10th century the Earls of Fife owned this area. Pilgrimages to St Andrew's remains in Fife had become popular and initially ran from Eilbottle. As trade grew, boats needed were too big to pull up the beach, so the ferry moved to a natural harbour at North Berwick. A church with hospice were built for pilgrims and, in 1150, a Cistercian nunnery to manage it. Scene of an infamous witch's coven it 1590, the church was abandoned after a storm tore off the eastern end in 1659, having been exposed by quarrying the 'red leck' for oven lining.

West Beach (3) *(take road to town, right onto beach)* Originally an island, the harbour was connected first by a wooden then a stone causeway near the restored RNLI lifeboat shed. The sand built up on either side to make this curved beach. At low tide, note the flat red rocks, remnants of a Devonian desert. The houses lining the beach were 19th © fishermen's homes, including the Low Quay. So fruitful was the local herring fishing that overspill boats from the harbour were pulled up onto the West Links. The Hope Rooms replaced the Dirleton Granary as a shelter for caddies; it still houses the local Youth Café. Ships would beach here and the massive stones at low tide are thought to have come as ballast.

Corner of High Street & Law Road looking East, 1890's

Westgate (4) *(up 2nd concrete steps, cross Forth St.)* This crooked street is where a town market was held. The pharmacy shop on the High Street was once stalls for three 'fleshers' (butchers) downstairs, with the town school room upstairs. From this point, Westgate, with its poorhouse, brewery and non-burghers, lay outside the town. In the other direction, the marked narrowing comes from centuries of encroachment on the street by greedy owners. The oldest survivor is a 18th century house at the corner of Law Road, following the old town boundary up the hill on the line of the Clarty Burn.

Kirk Ports (5) *(cross High St. into Law Road, then first left)* Built to replace the harbour's old kirk, this was the parish church from 1680 to 1888. It had a loft for each of the two landed gentry families of the Dalrymples of North Berwick and the Grant-Sutties of Balgone, the latter's family grave lies behind. Near the door, John Blackadder, who died in 1687 a prisoner on Bass Rock, lies under a huge slab. Following the once-narrow Kirk Ports to Quality Street leads to the heart of the town, with its Town Chambers and 18th century clock, across from which the tron or weighbridge once stood in the midst of the original (medieval) public market.

The Lodge (6) *(enter gate in railings, pass through arch)* This magnificent white building was until WW2 the residence of the Dalrymple local lairds. It consists of two separate residences—one for the laird and one for close family and was gifted to the town. Its grounds became the town park, recently restored to its original 18th century gardens and parkland layout. The house itself is now private residences. The 'wall' (or well) tower to the rear is the third-oldest building in the town, after the harbour kirk and the remains of the nunnery in Old Abbey Rd.

Quadrant (7) *(exit by aviary car park, right on East Rd)* In School Road stands the 1885 school that served until WW2, becoming the library and (closed) museum The East Road leads to East Links, known as the *Coo's Green*, where townspeople could graze their animals freely. Greenheads volcanic tuffs are a raised beach. On the hill jutting between the houses, a 13th century wooden 'castle' served as landward fortress for the Lauders of the Bass. The Quadrant itself, a delightful curve of late-19th century villas, was the boyhood summer home of Robert Louis Stevenson.

Melbourne Road with East Beach to the left, 1901

East Beach (8) *(cross onto beach, turn left)* The black rock back near Castle Hill inspired the scene in *Kidnapped* where the hero and Alan Breck elude the redcoats (and the shape of Fidra is reputed to have inspired *Treasure Island*). A fine terrace of Edwardian houses replaced a busy foundry that stood here until 1905. Past Coastguard cottages are a series of Victorian villas, summer boarding houses during the heyday of the 2-week, seaside holiday. In those days the 3,000 population would swell to 20,000. Mixed in are two fishermen's cottages that first stood here on a reclaimed sand spit that leads back to the harbour.

A Rough Chronology

400m BC (Devonian): In a dry, sandy desert the flat rocks of the West Beach are laid down.

200m BC (Carboniferous): Atlantic Ocean opens, tearing the crust; Bass Rock and Berwick Law erupt as volcanoes; many basaltic lava flows.

Ice Age(s): the land is scoured by East-flowing ice and the 'tail' of the Law forms from moraine.

c. 8,000 BC: with the ice is gone, plants and people arrive but sea levels are ~10m higher than now.

78 AD: Romans invasion leave Welsh Votadini— with a hillfort on the Law—in peace as allies.

606 AD: St Baldred dies at Tyninghame; remnants of Votadini/Goddodin succumb to Northumbria.

731 AD: Bishop Acca passes through *en route* to Fife, to save St Andrew relics from Vikings.

832 AD: Birth of saltire from cross-cloud formation that inspires English defeat at Athelstaneford

941 AD: Anulf the Dane sacks Tyninghame

1018: Malcolm II defeats English at Carham and Lothian is finally Scottish. By this time, many pilgrimages to St Andrews pass through here.

1150: Earls of Fife build first kirk and gift land to a nunnery that oversees pilgrim ferry & hospice.

1314: After Bannockburn, the Douglases are gifted lands to the East; build Tantallon in 1350.

1373: North Berwick's charter as a Royal Burgh.

1400-1513: Period of peace when trade with Hanseatic ports and Low Countries blooms. Harbour pier begun; a High Street develops.

1426: Lauders build their castle on Bass Rock

1505: John Major of Gleghornie receives Theology Doctorate from the University of Paris.

1577: Fenton Tower built to repel border raids.

1590: The crumbling kirk hosts a gathering of witches who cast spells to drown James VI.

1636: First lighthouse in Scotland on Isle of May.

1651: The crown buys the Bass Rock to use as a prison for Covenanters in its religious wars.

1659: A storm demolishes the old kirk, whose stone is 'recycled'. Reformation means no pilgrimages.

1664: Old kirk replacement built in Kirk Ports & Dalrymple family begin their long association.

1705: Binning Wood is planted by the 6th Earl of Haddington & Dalrymples buy Bass Rock.

1709: Whaling is popular; first jaw bone erected on Law and beeches planted to mark Act of Union.

1791: Population has grown to around 900. First granary at the harbour (now ELYC) as a store to ship out products of the agricultural revolution.

1803: Fencibles muster with 8 NCOs and 52 men to resist the French; Harbour Terrace granary built

1804: Stevenson family rebuilds the harbour; town sells Craiglieth to Dalrymples to pay for it all.

1832: North Berwick Golf Club founded. First school open in Market Place; town population: 1,834.

1850: North British Railway reaches the town; plans for an embankment to harbour never completed.

1861: Building boom: Royal Hotel built (replaced); RNLI establishes lifeboat station (closed 1925)

1876: Primary opens in School Road & Secondary School in Law Road (now Community Centre).

1882: Marine Hotel built/burns down/rebuilt; Astors build Quarry Court; Tennants build Hyndford

1883: Present St Andrew church started, new water supply piped in & gasworks moved out of town.

1895: Town's first firefighters; station is expanded; Galloway's pier opens for steamers in 1899.

1902: King Edward VII fêted on visit to King's Knoll; plants the tree now outside Burgh Chambers.

1915: East Fortune opens as an airship base; sends the R34 on first-ever transatlantic flight (1919)

1928: First council houses built in Lochbridge Road; Swimming pool & Pavilion built next to harbour.

1936: Playhouse cinema opens (replaced); heyday of bucket-&-spade holidays; population now 4,000.

1939: Present High School opens with 250 pupils; Army billeted on town includes Polish Armd. Div.

1969: RNLI re-establishes lifeboat service; NBTC subsumed into East Lothian six years later.

Family Day out

Dave Berry's amble
Was an informative ramble
Around N.Berwick town
He walked us through time
Through rain and through shine
Very proud of his glorious town

We came from Ilkley Moor
To climb North Berwick Law
We got so very much more
Than we bargained for
It's Great!

By The Fawcetts

Rugged Ralph

> The rugged Ralph
> Ran round
> The rugged rock

By Ralph Fawcett (8yrsold)

Wonderful William

> The wonderful William
> Went to wash his whacky washing
> When he was here

By William Fawcett (Ralph's Brother)

ESP

Guys get wise
Its "Enterprise"
Screen... is
Where you wanna be "Seen"!

Put it up there
Where we can all share
Limelight
Its outta sight!

By Enterprise Screen Team

Enterprise Screen was a generous sponsor during the Fringe by The Sea Festival.

3 Legged Dog

The 3-legged dog
Rode into the toon
Into the toon of MooseJaw

On a wobbly leg
To the sheriff he said
'Hey sheriff, I've come for ma paw'

By Jim Smith

The Spiegeltent

We watched it rise in t the sky
Gannets and puffins soaring by
Expectation was great,
We couldn't wait
Tickets were flying through the gate

At last we're here, under the crimson cover
With mirrors and balls helping us recover
From the wind and the rain
If we can get passes,
We'll definitely come again

By Alison Singleton

Waves

Crash against the shore
Silence
Ripples back
Leaving behind
Nothing
But
Bubbles

By folk in the queue

Oh, North Berwick

Oh North Berwick is a nice place
Everyone has a smile on their face.
The sea is so salty
it makes my legs go folty.
The street is so nice
It is a lovely treat.

By Hattie, Cathy & Charlot

Untitled

Being at the Fringe at the Sea
Makes me happy filled with glee
As I am one who gets to see
The many act perform at the sea

By Louise Melvin

The Big Yella Thing

My Holiday is coming to an end today
I am sad I have to go away
North Berwick is where I have lots of fun
But the big thing rising is the sun.

By Amy

In My Caravan

I have spent the summer at my caravan
I hope to do it even when I'm a man
But cos I'm young I just go out and play
And hope the rain... it stays away!

By Declan

Declan and Amy wrote together

Sea Shore

Sea Shore

Sun shinning on the sea,
Early morning stroll,
As happy as can be.

Sailing boat's are out,
Harbour walks in early evening,
Oh, what a beautiful sunset,
Running dog's playing in the waves
Ever Lasting memories.

By Diana .F

Our house in the middle of the street

There is always someone around our house
Chatting or drinking tea
Our house is a friendly place
When I come home at three

My room is pink and fluffy
It's the nicest room in the world
I like to play with my toys in there
Its perfect for this little girl

I like to come home to my mum and dad
My granny and grandad too
I like coming home to my house
I would like to invite you

By Emma-Lily Arbuddle (Age 9)

Rain

The rain is on again
It should go to Spain, so to speak
My roof has a leak, as I speak.
It is so depressing, quite stressing
I'll wait for the sun, then some fun.
I'll go down to the sea, in good old North B.
Can't think of any more, writing fingers are too sore.

Second verse next year!

Anonymous

N.O.R.T.H. B.E.R.W.I.C.K.

North Berwick – a quality place to be!

On the train to Edinburgh to see a show

Rain!

The Law – never yet attempted – maybe next year.

Hole in one – in my dreams!

Bass Rock – looks like a white muffin floating on the sea

Eating burgers and chips all day long

Rain again!

Wind – just what you expect from Scotland

Ice Cream – from Luca's van

Craigleith – I can see it from my window

Kids who never want to go home!

By Mark, Beth and Ella

The annoying boy

I was lying in my bed,
I could hear Nick shouting in my head
On and on and on ling a blooming gong,
While the waves crashed against the shore,
The annoying boy went on some more

By Chloe D'Inverno (age 8)

Berwick's Law

Stroll on the sand,
Bucket in hand,

Paddle in the sea,
Beautiful as can be.

Enjoy chocolate ice-cream,
Snooze in the sun - maybe even dream!

Savour fish 'n' chips,
Look out at ~~the safari of~~ ships.

Climb on the rocks,
Remember to take off your socks!

By Natasha D'Inverno

Sunstroke

The revenge of the rays
The worst of the best days
Streaming eyes, calamine lotion,
Aloe vera, scratched sunglasses,
Sandy sandwiches.
Its the third cheeseburger,
A good idea at the time
But then you feel sick

By David from Tippecanoe

Red Kite

Red kite, Jim, Girls and boys
Drawings and cutouts
Making our cartoon
To put on the net, then
Lunch at spiegeltent
Listening to music and
Writing my poem

By Lewision Cameron

Pride and Joy

Rufus is a little boy whose smile fills us with pride and joy

He's sometimes good, sometimes bad

That's because he is a lad.

The pride we have will grow and grow because he is the first you know.

Soon there will be another maybe a sister maybe a brother

Who knows what it will be for us doesn't matter

The main thing is that there will be the sound of patter patter

With love from
Grandma and Grandpa Kevan

Fred McCauley

Fred McCauley – oh by golly
Fringe by Sea is taking wings
Don't forget to bring the brolly
Barbara Dickson, what a dolly
Puts the wind beneath my THINGS!

Candian Jugg and Phil and Aly
Poetry, film, and Fats Sam's Band
Sula sails and dance so jolly
But don't forget to bring the brolly
Its summertime in auld Scotland.

Fish and chips or Thai Green Curry
Plenty nosh to fuel the soul
But mark OSTERIA – that's blue rib and
Food from heaven, Angelo!

But don't forget to bring the brolly
After all it just might rain
Quinton Jardine – next year Rankin?
Will make us all come back again.

By David Murdoch (age 101)
Apologies if I got some words wrong.
Tough reading yer 101 year old writing

The Quintessential North Berwick Limerick

There was a young girl from North Berwick
Who met a young man called derrick
They jumped into the Sea
But when she had a pee
Derrick had an hysteric

By Monica Loudon

Visiting

We're just o'er frae Florida
To paddle in yer pool
We thought it wud be warm
But it was cool
But if truth be told
It was cold.

By McGonagle

The Sun in North Berwick

Fun in the sun
A likely thing to say
Rare to North Berwick,
It could happen any day

Make the most of it
Whilst its here to stay,
Because tomorrow
It may have gone away.

By Helen

My Favoraite Place

My favoraite place

My favoraite place in all the World, is Noth Berwick by the Sea, I love it because it makes me feel so free beside the Sea.

I love the Sea,
I love the Sand,
I love the rocks as well.
It's just because the Sea Side has me under neth it's spell.

By Lauren Dickson

AHOY! – North Berwick

AHOY! – NORTH BERWICK.

When I visit North Berwick by the sea,
It's a pirate that I most wish to be.
With an eye-patch, a dagger,
a skull and cross bones on my cheek.
Oh, if only my holiday was longer than just one week!

By Gulliver Dickson

Fringe by the Sea

FRINGE BY THE SEA

While sitting in the Spiegel tent
A nice young man was most intent
A poem I should write
What can I say
A wonderful day
For one and all to enjoy
Come back next year
And give a cheer
To the festival fringe by the sea

By Mary Buglass

Maisie's Boat

Nana and Grandad went on a boat
   Toot Toot
They saw stars
   Toot Toot
Maisie's boat

By Maisie Mclachlan (aged 2)

Dictated to mummy and daddy
Also known as Janet & Malky McLachlan

Simply the Best

✱ SIMPLY THE BEST ✱

There was an old lady who lived by the Sea,
She couldn't help but have a nice cup of tea,
She was an avid fan of sun and sand,
She met a lovely man who had one hand.

One day she went for a swim,
And ran into her old friend g Jim,
They spent the day collecting shells,
then Jim told her that she smells.

She felt so sad she sat and began to cry,
All she had wanted to do was try,
that was the end of, poor old Jim.
~~She ran over threw him in the bin~~!
he ended up in the bin!

By Darren & Amanda

Off key

Plaintive, nasal & overamplified
The guitarist frightens even the gulls.

By Bill Waugh

From Submarine to the Moon

I would like to go to the moon
And I wish it was very soon
Flying about in a rocket
With lots of sweets in my pocket

By Jack Nicklaus

The Big Tent " North Berwick Harbour

It's big and white
It's like the Tardis
I came for lunch and the Open Mic
Lots of guitars and songs

Colourful windows
Good BBQ chicken
And I'm not just saying that
Because I don't want to be rude

And that's the big tent
I hope it stays forever

By Owen Mackle (age 8)

Hugh's 2nd Ditty

Fringe by the sea
The best place to be
Lots of fun
For everyone

By Hugh Trevor

NB Shore

North Berwick shore
I've been there before
a sea so blue
I find it true
the sound of the waves
a play in the caves
a play on the sand
a great day planed
a bbQ
some thing to chew
this is our beach
it's easy to Reach

By Kieren Shields

Bunfight

Launches Launching
Bellies Paunching
Comedians Huddling
Peddlars Guddling
Tourists Swarming
Weather Warming
Teenagers Posing
Old Dossers Dozing
Beer Taps Gushing
PR Types Rushing
Everyone Pushing
Quiet types Shooshing
Thespians Emoting
Fosters judges Voting
Footlights are trying
Some on-stage dying
The good and the bad
The ugly and sad
The funny and tragic
Some crap and some magic
The festival fringe
The wild late night binge
3 weeks of the year
God help us – Its here

By Alison Craig

North Berwick

NORTH BERWICK

"It's great in North Berwick
Singing for Eric,
Spiegeltent too,
And what a view!"

POEMCATCHER.COM
This fabulous poem is donated with love and may happily be published
Poet's Name: BARBARA DICKSON

By Barbara Dickson

Raj

We like to chill at the beach
Go to the church
And have a preach...
LOL JK we steal and
Drink and fight according
To the police on a Friday
Night.

My Mendez

See

We came to the fringe by the Sea
To see what there was to see
We found singers and musicians
Storytellers and Comedians
Which suited us down to a tee

By Neil Hynd

North Berwick Highland Games

    On an early August weekend
We hope the dark, heavy clouds suspend
Their plans to rage and their angst to pour
For a day like this needs dreekit weather no more

The air is rich with tunes so complete;
Melodies dance to a clever beat
Bass drums conduct their heavy tread
A sound so deep and strong -but don't be misled
Listen close and hear the mystical drone
Which whispers ancient secrets
The clans of Scotland once told

The pipe bands come from far and wide
All proudly wearing a kilt with delight
Whose vivid colours originate from a fine Scotsman
Who perhaps once lived as a MacDonald, a Stewart or a MacLaughlan

However the bands are not the only travellers -
They're accompanied by their bonnie dancers
Their vibrant tartans swing and sway
With each graceful hop and step they take
As they perform their highland fling for the judges' sake

The heavies with their muscles so strong
Lift weights and throw the Scots hammer long,
The caber they toss to 12 o'clock high
With 20ft of caber into the sky

From the year 1996, a gentleman, who goes by the name of Starr
Produced an event that attracted thousands from afar
I'm sure if you go to North Berwick Highland Games,
I have no doubt,
You're sure to have a Champion Scottish Day Out.

By Luisa Starr

Jelly Belly

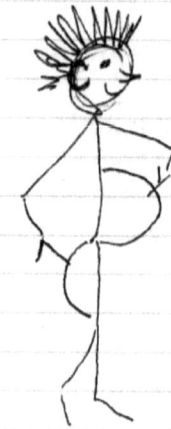

JELLY IN MY BELLY
JELLY IN MT TUM
THIS IS MY BELLY
AND THIS IS MY BUM!

By Judith

The Place to be

Fringe by the Sea
is the place to be

When the Spiegeltent is full of wine
We're all having a brilliant time

Barbara Dickson, Eddie Reader
           Ali Bain & all the rest
They're all singing & playing at their best
But then
I've been captures by the man
           With the sunglasse hat
To write a poem about all that
Which is really difficult when you're
           Pissed as a rat

By Anne M

Fishy Face Rap

(Must be rapped)

Swimming up
Swimming down
Swimming all around town
Here comes mister fishy man
With his fishy face
Watch out or he'll come for you
Stupid fishy face!

I can't swim.

Xxx
Love you

By Osian Edwards-Muthu and Michael Lewis (Age 17)

Morning World

That's what poetry's all about
How it lies on a aparticular person's shoulders
How they cope
How it fits
Old granny jumper
Corduroy jacket
Wearing confidence and flow
Bloody seagulls
Kept awake
Turning circle
Little
The pint is coming
Towards East Bay
South of somewhere
North

By John Higgins

Poetical snippets of a conversation on High Street

The Sea by Camper

As I open the door, the smell of the sea tickles my nose,
The sound all around,
The wind makes me feel alive
A feast for all the senses
Most of all sight
Ever changing glorious wild sea
Thank you for allowing me to share
A tiny part of you.

By Carole Racionzer

"Fringe Fun"

      Sea and Sand who needs the sun
           At fringe by the sea
      We're having fun

      Rhythm and Blues
           And lots of soul
      These late nights
           will take their toll

        Five action packed days
       And nights of fun
      Fringe by the Sea
         Something for everyone

By Jane

Getting the Fringe benefits

The weather's not good
But it doesn't dampen the mood
It's time for some glee
At the Fringe by the Sea

From far and wide they travel
In various venues to marvel
As artists perform their works,
There could be a few larks.

The final verdict, as they all cheer,
'It's bigger and better than last year!'

By Ian Walker

The reluctant performer

Will this audience be kind?
I tell myself I don't mind.
I think I'm a wit
But to them I might be a twit.
This is new verse
I really should rehearse.
I wish they'd go away
And come back another day.
I'm all of a quiver,
It's now or never.
I hope they don't think it's a con
After all, the show must go on.
Later, the sheer relief.
Oh, good grief
It's all over
And I don't need to run for cover.
Just a nervous pause
Then there's laughter and applause.

By Ian Walker

S.A.L.T.Y.

S is for the salty air
    That fills your heart with glee

A is for the anglers with
    Their fishy sodden sea

L is for the life and song
    From tales of ships at bay

T is for the tale I tell
    Of another one to say

Y is for the yearning
    To return another day

By Jonathan Bell

Sitting by the Sea

Sitting By The Sea

I see the sea,
I hear the waves,
I smell the salt in the sea air,
I feel the sun beating down on my skin,
While the cool breeze makes me tingle,

I watch the boats on the horizon,
They are so colourful and hypnotic,
Dancing to the rhythm of the sea.
There is something about being by the sea,
that makes you feel so free.

Poet's Name: Miss Blossom

By Miss Blossom

Rant

Statistics, Statistics

They really take the biscuits

Anon

Get Up

Ditch the sulks and burn the scowl
Raise the standard, grab a towel
The beach is waiting, the sea is warm
North Berwick seaside goes down a storm
A west coast boy I still may be
But I love it here — and fresh air's free!

By Alistair Wilson

Love& Money

Love, money, money love
Biggest house, Smallest loan
Blue skies shining bright above
Set the scene, set the tone

Love my bag, leather sheen
£500, now don't be mean
Car: price of a house
Yet, everyone a dirty louse

Wash the windows, weed the lawn
Scrub the patio, super clean
Sneaky, sneaky internet porn
Diet, diet, live the lean

Love, money, money, love.

By Victoria Knight

Life in Marly Green

20 houses

Lots of folk

Hot air ballons

Big big boats

Mad neighbours

Great friends

Grow old happy

Party time

By Sally

The Spiegel Prayer

>I'm in a booth
>>'wi and offie drooth
>
>Hope I don't fall off
>>The step forsooth!

By Jan Williams

By The Sea

How light, winter dawn
Croaking Gannets – Yawn, yawn

Bass Rock, cold; remote
Sula- sickening & rocky boat

N.B. fry, chips and fish
Lots of taste but fat content pish!

Can't park the car
Gullane's too far

Festival by the Sea
Hey! Glee, Glee, Glee.

By Victoria Knight

Saturdays

There were 3 ladies in N.B.
Who loved their life by the sea
They coffeed & shopped
They drank and they scoffed
And lived the life of Rile-ee!

By Sally

North Berwick

By the Sea in North Berwick,
On the beach and in the town,
See the faces all around,
Whilst they're having fun.

Sometimes the weather is glorious,
Sometimes it is awful,
But whatever the weather,
We'll always be by the sea.

By Sophie Falk

Del Sol

> Kids Jumpy + clappy
> Makes mummy happy
> Orchestra delsol
> We have a ball
> North Berwick – seaside heaven
> FBTS – see you in 2011!

By Kathryn Hewitt

Harr

> The harr rests on the breaking waves,
> The sands are clear and clean and hushed
> The silence echoes in the caves
> And nothing here has ever rushed
>
> For days the islands hide away,
> Though they still stand, alone at sea
> The Bass, Craigleith, the Lamb and May
> And white sails shelter in their lea
>
> But the sun will make his long return
> Shores of Fife once more in view
> And on the cost the sand will burn
> A seaside summer through and through

By Captain Hugo

Alan's Poem

When midnight comes at 12 o'clock
I lie in bed and think a lot
I think about the day to come
As well as what has been and gone

By Captain Hugo

Local Input

I've come a' the way frae Pathhead
And I have-nae a rime in mae heed!
But ne'er say die
I'll gie it a try
To see what ye think of my screed!

By Sheila MacBrayne

Bass Rock Birds

> B for Birds
> They sit an the spikey edges
> White and splashy
> Waah, Waah, lod and shouty
> And a little bit stinky!

By Joseph Gerald (age 3 ½)

High Times

> High tides predicted
> High times expected
> High times ensued
>
> Eddi was good
> Phil was brill
> But Maggie was
> My darling
> - And Pauline left
> me breathless not
> 'shameless'

By John Shaw

Seashell

What do you hear little one
    With the shell t your ear?
Do you hear white horse jumping
    Or monsters to fear?
Do you hear gannets squawking
    And waves lapping near?
Do you see the sails flapping
    Across the waters so clear?
Whatdo you hear little one
    With the she to your ear
Tell me the stories, my little dear.

By Carol
North Berwick Day Centre

We stayed in a flat...

Called by the sea
near a Place named Melbourne, down under
the Burgh and the Seabird bluff
where the Firth furls forth and the Firth
faces north to its south-facing shore
in a Berwick north of Berwick
by an islet that May and a rock
of Bass in a shoal of isles
where the Links are linked
by Quality Street
and the hill is Law.

By Will Daunt

Tippecanoe

All of us at Tippecanoe
Work in a town with award winning loos,
North Berwick has been sunny and faire
The sea, the sand and the salty air

Fringe by the sea was a great success,
Poemcatchers, artists and fancy dress,
Next year will be bigger and better
Provided our weather gets sunny not wetter!

By Amber Hunter
At Tippecanoe

*Tippecanoe is a beautiful store at
the end of high street (No.1)
They stock amazing things - Like a book called SALTY*

Another poem found

There wis five ladies fae Dundee
Who came to holiday by the sea
The lights of Kirkcaldy were a-blinking
Just as the fishing boat was sinking
'Help! Help! was the cry o'er the waves
And all the sailors' souls were saved
By the 5 ladies oh so brave
Hooray! Hooray! Hooray!

[Apologies to Wm T McGonagall]

By The Famous Five

Keep Smiling Through

Uniforms, gasmasks, every nuance of war
Vera Lynn, Coward, VD and more
Evoked the memories, tugged at the heart
Remembering families bomb-ripped apart

Emotional heights and desperate depths
Revealed in the diaries that some folk kept…

Songs from the Forties
The force on sorties
We'd really like more, please

Whatever your age, whatever you do
Don't miss the show "Keep Smiling Through"

By Anne Fraser

Jean Florette

Intimate story in intimate venue
Jean de Florette was exquisite and sad
French country life with a greedy plot
A feast for the eye – its got the lot!

By Anne Fraser

Raise your hem FC Ukelele

A veritable feast of talented players
Amid the sandcastles, sailing boats, sea
Capture and entertain people on holiday
North Berwick's provided a "boquet garni"

Well done "Fringe by the Sea"

By Anne Fraser

CATCH OF THE DAY

Mushrooms

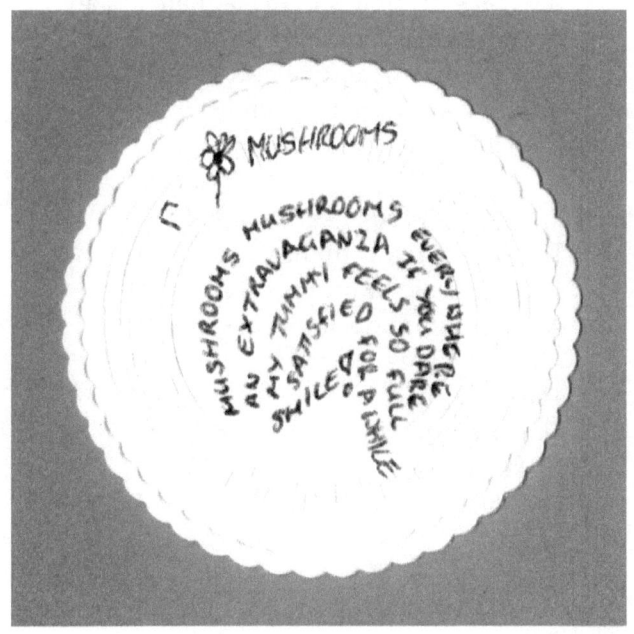

By Jane Lees

My Honey

I am a busy bee, unlucky me,
All my life's work is for nothing, no point
in all this lugging and pugging
they take my honey to make them money.
My honey is like running water
All this time I'm getting hotter
Its weird, they think its funny
I like it thick, they like it runny.

I'm getting tired I need a nap, they
Try to swat me with their cap
Their caps are swatting, killing things
And before I know it my stinger stings
And so I realize
That's the last
Time I will
Make honey.
My honey

By Eve Walker

First Hotdog in Space

Eating a hotdog outside Spiegel
Reminded me of my dog that's a beagle
My dog got eaten by an eagle
The second dog in Space I thought it
The first dog was Leica and he bought it
- A real hot dog –

By Andrew, Fraser & Grandad

Toast to a "Steak Bake"

Oh you poor and timorous pastrie
Lying on 'Greggs' shelf looking so tasty
Filled with gravy and mechanically extracted meat
My mouth waters at such a sumptuous treat
With one bite my mouth fills with pleasure
My taste buds explode with your hidden treasure
My 5-A-Day can wait another hour
My lunchtime filled with your SteakBake power.

By Ken Hutchinson

Meat

Pork is the meet of kings
Eat it and your soul will sing
This is why men come to baguette express
And read the local news press!
They serve pork on the silver platter
And this truly is what matters

By Kieran Robson

BEE & FAMILY

On a rainy day poem-catching in N.B. I was rescued by three angels.
    One offered me a place to dry my clothes.
    One gave me an umbrella
    One inspired me to keep going.

While drying my clothes.
I found warmth in the soup and in the community that welcomed me at The Beacon.
I was given my first poem for the day.
I sold a book.
My dampness dried. My mood lifted.

I was sent on a treasure hunt, to find a poetic pot of gold...
A 91year old poet named Bee.

It was treasure hunt that was going to have to wait.
Open Mic was due to begin in Spiegeltent.
20 poems were written in that one hour in the tent.
I was given an umbrella.

The treasure hunt resumed, leading me to the day-centre.
Arriving in the middle of a delightful fiddle & keyboard performance. I found myself on centre stage.

Poems revealed beneath the kilt.
And Bee was found for tea.
An Inspiring tea.
Connecting me to the N.B. poets and writers group...
And a many other delightful encounters.

My week went from wet to wonderful.
                                    A grateful PoemCatcher

Untitled

"Far –away places with strange-sounding names" –
That was a song that was sung
By fantastic fellow or fabulous dames,
When all my world was young.
Kilimanjaro and Kalamazoo,
Hearts left in San Francisco –
How did they get there? And what did they do?
Now all <u>we</u> have is the "disco"

Still, all you wanderers, we do have a place
With sea, sun and treats atmospheric.
Run down to the beach, or up to the Law…
There's nowhere on Earth like North Berwick!!

By M.E. Moskal
10.7.10

"Summer!"

What a summer this has been –
Rain, and wind, and glaur –
Makes you wonder what's the point
Of living any more!

I just feel, of arsenic
I'll take a hearty quaff
And then I'll walk into the sea
Until my hat floats off.
Please don't try to stop me –
You know you're only jealous,
I'll live among the mermaids
And the handsome young merfellows!
On second thoughts, I'd miss my treats –
A cheery cuppa tea,
A little flat that's warm as toast
And views of Law and sea.
Ho hum…I'd better simmer down
And settle for N.B.

By M.E. Moskal

Moving

Move to the country? Move to the City?
Move me to tears, move me to pity
Pawn to Queen 3, Knight to king 7?
Move down to hell, or upwards to heaven?
What is the point of my moving at all,
Whether I run, or steadily crawl?
All that awaits me – a flat with a view,
Tow rooms with a bed, a kitchen, a loo
Move to the North?
      Move to the West?
This flat will do me
      And HERE I WILL REST…

By ME Moskal
12.6.09

Glitter

"All that glitter is not gold" –
Very often we've been told.
The tie-pin in the lover's tie
Is not as sparky as his eye.

"Oliver – just see them gleam"
Fagan said, his voice like cream,
Drooling o'er his ill-got treasure
(funny way to get your pleasure!)

I'd much rather get my raves
From watching sunshine on the waves,
Listening to the seabird's voice,
That's <u>my</u> shining glittery choice.

By M.E.. Moskal
May 2010

The Day Centre, North Berwick

If you're wondering what to do –
Visit friends? Go to the Zoo?
If you're bored with usual ploys
(find the T.V. just a noise)
Fetch your coat and make your way
To the Centre for the day.

There you'll find some friendly folks,
Making coffee, making jokes,
Lunches, too are on the menu –
It's a splendid chummy venue.
Music, talks and photo shows,
Films and teas and – goodness knows.

There is something at the Centre
Made to suit all those who enter!

By M.E. Moskal
Spring 2010

Far out to Sea

(By Bee's granddaughter, Zoe)

When I look far out to sea
I see the sea and she sees me.
I dance amongst her rippling waves
And glide on through her reefs and caves.

When I look far out to sea
She slowly seems to swallow me.
Engulfed in sheeny waters blue
I slide and soar as fishes do

When I look far out to sea
I see the sea and she sees me.
But if the sea could not see me
I really don't think it could be
Quite so thrilling
Quite so free
As seeing Sea when she sees me

At one with the sea I'm strong
For i know this is where I belong
And so here I'll remain
In your salty domain
With each whispering wave i feel safe
Lost in the blue
Of you

By Zoe Moskal Guy

Written when she was 11, Now 18.
Listen to the song version on her album
ZASS:join the dots at www.zassmuic.co.uk

Nibble

The sea comes in, the sea goes out
    And in, ad infinitum
And if you dip your toes in it
A jelly fish'll bite 'em.

By Tina Moskal

GOLF

The Great Game of Golf

We put our balls on the tee
While waiting with glee
For eh best blow of the 21st century

Straight in the hole
We achieved our goal
It was over to fast
We wanted it to last
Disappointment all round
It only cost us two pound
At North Berwick golf club
Of, well. Off to the pub
With the boys
Oh, the joys.

By Charile Yates and Ryan Duncanson

Golf in the Sun

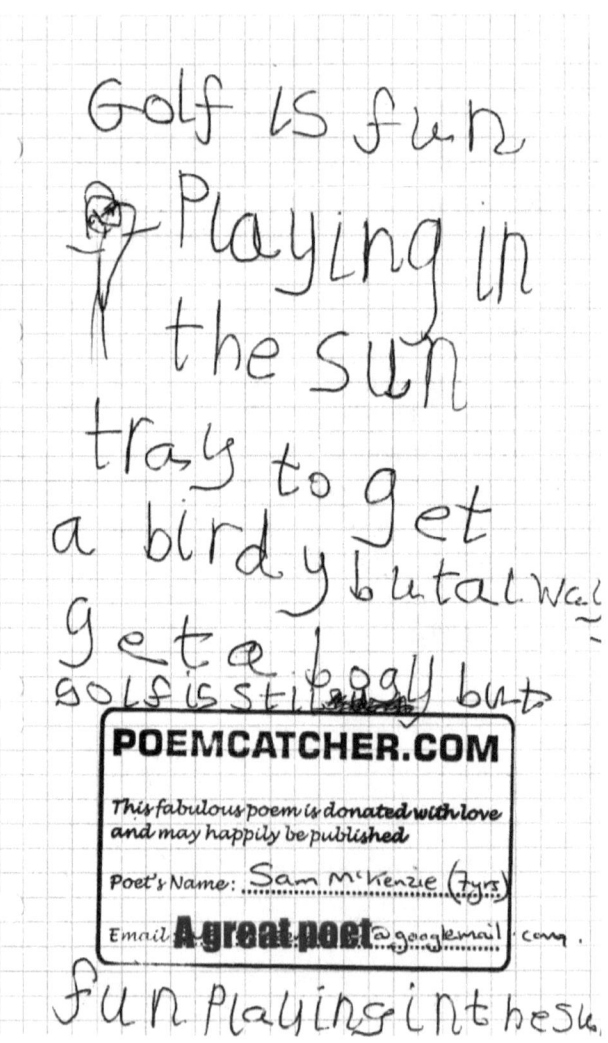

Golf is fun
Playing in the sun
Tray to get a birdy but always
Get a bogy but
Golf is still
Fun playing in the sun

By Sam McKenzie (age 7)

Golf

A wisp of green
a bit of air
along a row
No longer field
presents itself
and forms with sand and waving grasses
a new challenge
as it does each day
I pass this way
to meet my challenge
and enjoy the day

By Rick McMillian

ROMANCE

David and Amy's Page

Down by the sea,
Is where you can find,
Plenty for thee,
To entertain you mind

On North Berwick Beach we first held hands
Fifteen months ago down on the sand
Now that man's going to marry me
Down on the beach by the sea

By David and Amy

Charlie

Sitting by the sea
Right here, you and me
10 years ago, naive together
Now looking at the sky
Contemplating the weather
Looking at you now,
Seeing how you've grown
Wondering what could have been
I guess we'll never know

By Hazel Herriot

*These two were childhood sweethearts
And were inspired to write after hearing
David and Amy's poem*

Tulips

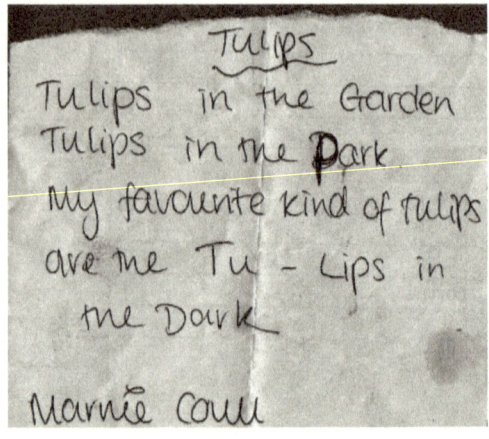

Tulips in the garden
Tulips in the park
My favourite kind of tulips
Are the Tu-Lips in the dark

By Marnie C

A poem to writing

Stay with me,
My love,
Until the stars have blinked their last,
Wherever on this Earth you walk
I will arouse, excite, inspire,
My True Valentine, My one true fire

By Stephan Johnstone

This place

I won't frequent this place again,
ever.
For in this place he and I
never
held hands, kissed, or sighed
together
We walked and talked of other things
discretely
because he sensed my need was him
completely.

The sun went down.
The child he held was crying
for suns which die.
Yet saw our spirits flying
across the beach to meet the sea.
Tide turning.
The ebbs and floes of friendship
are worth learning.

One love relinquished,
so my heart will beat
a deeper love
like sand beneath our feet.
Golden. Firm.
Though soft and yielding, ever.
He takes my hand.
I smile.
We walk together.

By Jenny Fardell

OUTGOING TIDE

Nap time

Winded yarns and salty tales,
Chips and cheese and seagull wails
Vinegar wafts on salty streams
I taste it still on lips, in dreams
When night it falls on seagull scream
And then my mind with angst to quench
Breathes in still on seaward bench
And then my eyes and stars they fall
And I know nothing at all

By James Murray

Write another poem here...

If you're feeling inspired, go ahead and write, doodle, draw, create, play...

List of Poets

Alastair (age 8), 18
Alex Ralston, 16
Ali Buchanan, 31
Alison Craig, 67
Alison Singleton, 43
Alistair Wilson, 83
Amber Hunter, 94
Amy, 45
Andrew Newman, 19
Andrew, Fraser & Grandad, 101
Anne Fraser, 96, 97
Anne M, 73
Barbara Dickson, 68
Bill Waugh, 63
Captain Hugo, 89, 90
Carol, 92
Carole Racionzer, 76
Charile Yates, 115
Chloe D'Inverno, 50
Darren & Amanda, 62
Dave Berry, 30, 34
David and Amy, 120
David Berry, 27
David Farmery, 14
David Murdoch, 24, 55
Declan, 45
Diana .F, 46
Emma-Lily Arbuddle, 47
Enterprise Screen Team, 42
Eve Walker, 100
folk in the queue, 43
Grandma and Grandpa Kevan, 54
Gulliver Dickson, 59
Hattie, Cathy & Charlot, 44
Hazel Herriot, 121
Helen, 57
Hugh Trevor, 25, 65
Ian Walker, 78, 79
Jack Nicklaus, 64
James Murray, 126
Jane, 77
Jane Lees, 99
Jenny Fardell, 124
Jim Smith, 42
John Dory, 23
John Higgins, 75
John Shaw, 91
Jonathan Bell, 80
Joseph Gerald, 91
Judith, 72
Kathryn Hewitt, 89
Ken Hutchinson, 102
Kieran Robson, 103
Kieren Shields, 66
Lauren Dickson, 58
Lauren Watt, 21
Lewision Cameron, 53
Louise Melvin, 44

Luisa Starr, 71
Lyle Crawford, 12
Maisie Mclachlan, 61
Mark, Beth and Ella, 49
Marnie C, 122
McGonagle, 56
Mendez, 69
Michael Lewis, 74
Miss Blossom, 20, 81
Monica Loudon, 56
Natasha D'Inverno, 51
Neil Hynd, 69
North Berwick Day Centre, 92
Osian Edwards-Muthu, 74
Owen Mackle, 64
Ralph Fawcett (8yrsold), 41
Rick McMillian, 118
Ronald Peebles, 15
Ryan Duncanson, 115
Sally, 85, 87
Sam McKenzie, 117
Sheila MacBrayne, 90
Sophie Falk, 88
Stephan Johnstone, 123
The Famous Five, 95
Tina Moskal, 113
Victoria Knight, 84, 86
Will Daunt, 93
William Fawcett, 41
Zoe Moskal Guy, 112

OTHER POEMCATCHER BOOKS

QUAKE Built from Nothing
Made in 4 days, begging for poems on the pavements of St Andrew's, as an unofficial one-man fringe event for StAnza poetry festival 2010

BALLS from the Queue (Game, Set and Match)
A trilogy of tennis poems captured at Wimbledon 2010 in the infamous queue for centre court tickets.

FUNGUS Poems
Mushroom and fungal poetry written by the world's leading scientists at the 9th international Mycology Conference in Edinburgh

www.ingramcontent.com/pod-product-compliance
Lightning Source LLC
Chambersburg PA
CBHW031254290426
44109CB00012B/579